1912

Poems of Time, Place & Memory

1912

Poems of Time, Place & Memory

Kary Hess

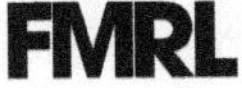

1912: Poems of Time, Place & Memory

Copyright © 2022 Kary Hess
All rights reserved.

First Edition

ISBN: 978-1-7379492-1-3

Library of Congress Control Number: 2022935485

Book cover, interior design, and illustrations by Kary Hess.
Cover photo by Murray Rockowitz.

Special thanks to Jonah Raskin, Cindy Shearer, Carolyn
Cooke, Clee Ferris, Mandy Steward, Julie Reid, Debra
Wohrman, and Audy Davison.

Manufactured in the United States of America.

FMRL
40 4th St. No. 111
Petaluma, CA 94952
fmrl.com

For Daedalus

Contents

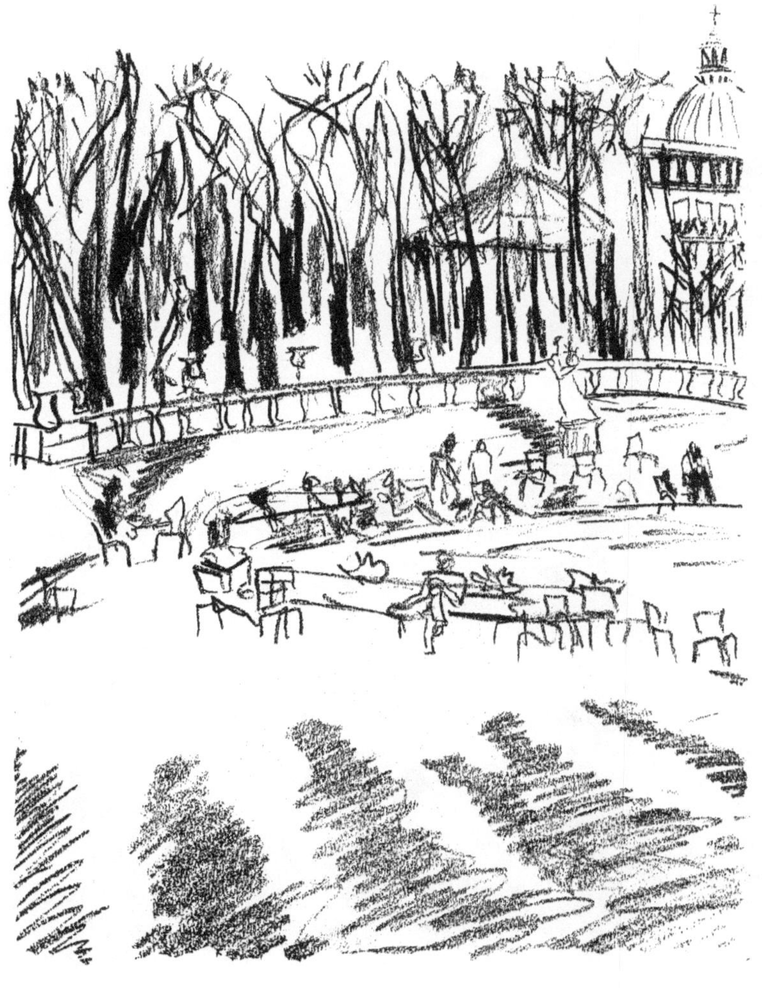

Prologue

Memories are art. They morph and shift in the mind of the person remembering and the culture one is immersed within. What I experience today is not what I will remember tomorrow, and it's definitely not what I will remember twenty years from now.

Our remembrances are like that, one of a kind in each moment and not what I might want to call "accurate" in my recollection, even if I think they are. But it doesn't matter. Because what I actually remember with the details of these moments is how I felt and how it changed me, not whether it was the Petaluma or the Novato library where I permanently borrowed that book when I was nine...or ten.

I've lived in three places: Paris, France; Provo Utah; and Petaluma, California. I only lived in Paris for four months in 1989, during the country's bicentennial, so it was truly a moment in time with a particular character. If I were to return today, the only thing that might feel the same is the complex and overwhelming scent at the Chatelet Métro stop. But I know I can't really ever go back to the experience I had in Paris by going back to Paris.

Utah was my home for three years, long enough for some of my memories there to conflict with the memories of others. During that time, I lived in at least six different apartments and socialized with dozens of people. The seasonal changes added additional veils of sensation to our experiences, from the freezing white winters to the red-hot summers.

It's enjoyable and useful to relive past moments with the people I shared them with. It leads to a more intricate picture of events as we recall our similar versions of that time, but with an emphasis on different — and often forgotten — details.

And thirty years is plenty of time to alter memory. My friend Tamara, in Utah, added photos from a road trip that she wasn't on into her photo album, because she thought she was there. It took a bit of convincing to persuade her that she was not with us on that road trip! But in the end, the photos reminded her of her own memories of that time in our lives so does it really make much difference?

When I moved back to Petaluma, California in 1993, experience and memory became even more complex. Because I grew up in Petaluma, and also have lived here as an adult for most of my life, there are multiple layers of remembrance for me in the places throughout this area. Conversely, there are many forgotten moments that live embedded in the landscape and in the memories of others — however they remember them — and of course in some cases those moments are just gone forever.

I've always been compelled to fill sketchbooks with writing and drawings, so the stories I tell myself about the past are augmented by that record. Sometimes, I'm surprised when I read a passage from an old journal and discover that how I remember something today wasn't the same as what I myself wrote down at the time.

For this book, I perused some of the journals from my youth and wrote these poems based on a combination of what I remembered and what I found there, so maybe they are more "accurate" than they might have been had I not kept journals. The drawings are all from the various notebooks I kept during those times.

April 2022
Petaluma, California

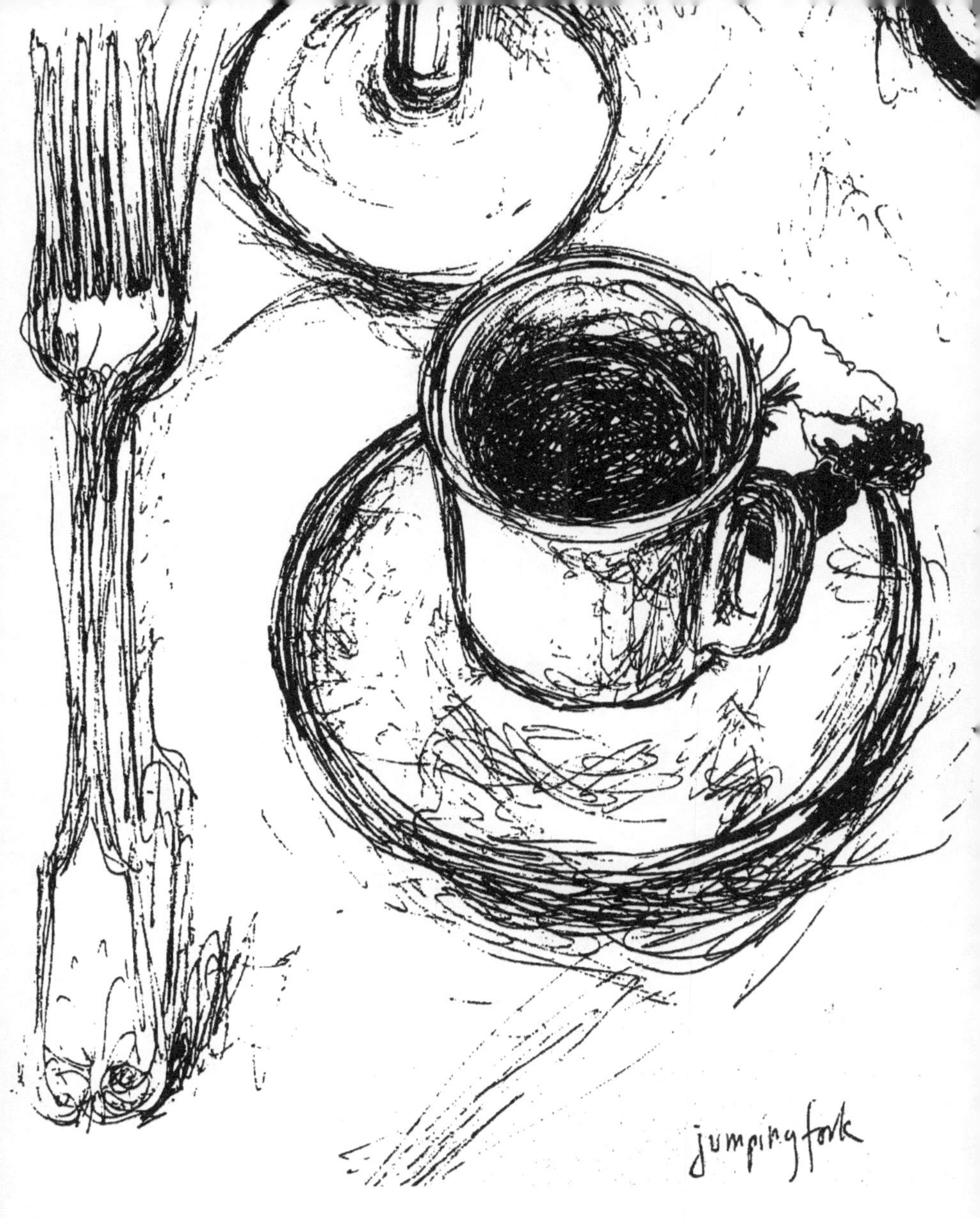
jumping fork

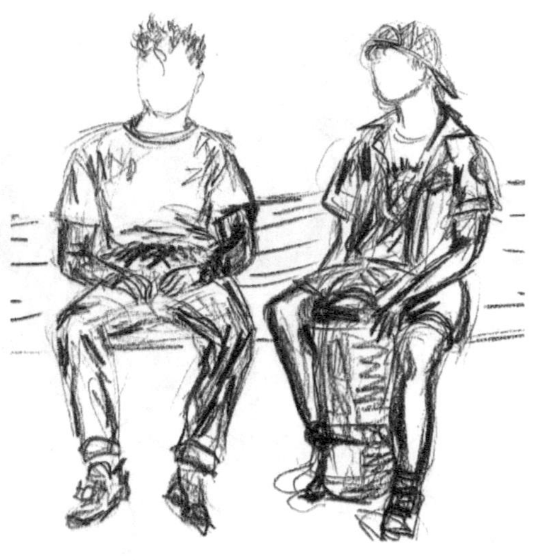

During my childhood, we kids rode our bikes to school and spent entire days and summers outside in the woods, at the swimming pool, or at the movies. Our downtown theater, in particular, offered a curated selection of foreign and art films, along with science fiction, fantasy favorites, and adult films — one of which we accidentally saw when our parents thought it was a kids' movie because it was animated. It was a time when children were without a lot of adult supervision, as evidenced by the name given to our generation, X, an unknown factor.

Generation X

The Scorcher

This is no suburban cul-de-sac moment.
We live on a dirt road in the country
with gravel in the driveway
and I am trying to ride a bike.

Try riding in gravel over potholes
when you are six years old.
But I don't know.
I think I'm just not very good
at riding a bike.

At the turn of the century
(the twentieth century),
the bicycle was a new invention.
They called it the Scorcher
it was so fast.

But today the only scorcher is this summer day
and I'm trying again and again
to ride this damn bike
so I can ride to school instead of walking
the two miles down winding country roads
to the one-room schoolhouse
when second grade begins in the fall.

My dad supportively holds the back
of the rickety red-and-white contraption
while I move the rusty pedals with my sandaled feet
handlebars all over the place.
Then the crunch of gravel as the bike turns in front
and falls over again and again.

Now I am riding pretty good
until I panic and freeze
at the end of the driveway
and crash right into the barbed-wire fence.
I get up and keep riding numb
my flesh blood and fabric of my ripped skirt
left behind in the sharp wires.
My body is scraped and bleeding
by the end of the day
but I'm riding the bike.

And when the warm part of fall arrives
I'm riding home from school
on the three-inch-wide asphalt shoulder when
a hay truck whisks past me.
And light as a feather
the wind from the truck

lifts me off the road.
My bike and I slowly float
into a gulley lined with rocks and weeds.

When I open my eyes
from the warm scratchy ground
I look up at the sky
clouds drifting past
blinding sun
the buzzing of insects
and trills of red-winged blackbirds
on wires
as I lie there bleeding in the ditch
for as long as I feel like.

I leave another part of myself there
and pick up my bike
keep riding home
blood trailing behind me from
elbows, head and knees and
a two-inch gash on my leg
already starting to scab over.

I still have the scar.

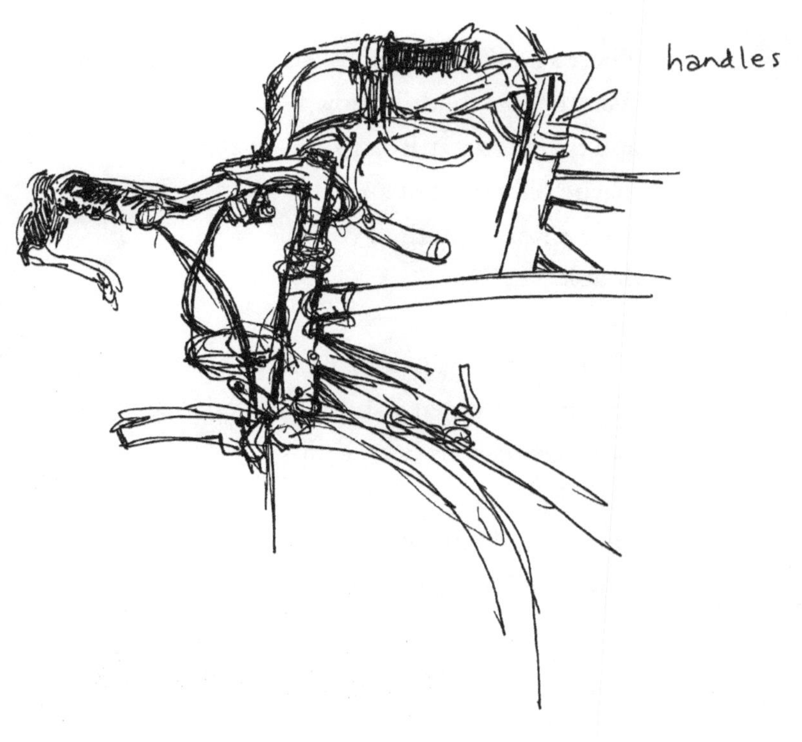

handles

The Plaza Theater

There's a plant in the broken drinking fountain.
We watch its tendrils grow longer all summer
and there is a particular smell in this place
maybe old popcorn and
the dust of a hundred years
or at least sixty.

Velvet curtains a box of Cracker Jacks
up the stairs down a short carpeted aisle
partly cracked art deco lamps
dimly light our way
straight to the front row balcony
so we can look down over the edge.

My friends and I are there
for the science fiction triple feature
so our moms can please just have
five or six hours without us
to go antiquing or day drinking.

We tumble into creaking wooden seats
dirty from decades of use
But it's dark so we don't know
and we don't care
about dirt

or whether our parents
want time without us.

In this dark self-contained world
I never once think about what might be
behind that screen.

Because it's all creatures and triffids and aliens
and French men and My Fair Lady and the Beatles
and dark crystals and mysterious islands and
whatever strange world illuminates
the front of that screen
today.

Most of the time we don't even know
what we'll find until we get there.
And neither do our parents, really.

That day, we open our Cracker Jacks boxes
and trade prizes in the shadows.
Somehow Shannon gets
all the joke books
and so we gang up against her
to take them back
before the movie begins.

Christine's Café

I'm drawing again.
The lines comfort me, I belong here,
my hair dyed black at the ends and in my eyes.

The shapes and lines from my subjects become
a way to connect with
my place.

There's a cigarette between my lips and
my charcoal pencil moves over the sketchbook page.
Sean's hair, Jane's plaid skirt, Lauren's leather jacket.

I am compelled.
Charlie's skateboard, Debbie hugs her friend
a circle of girls lying on their stomachs legs bent.

The old post office across the street
café to my right
Repo Man playing tonight at the Palace.

Then we're drinking coffee in Christine's Café
smoking again at our table by the window
a table cluttered with the excitement of
our potential.

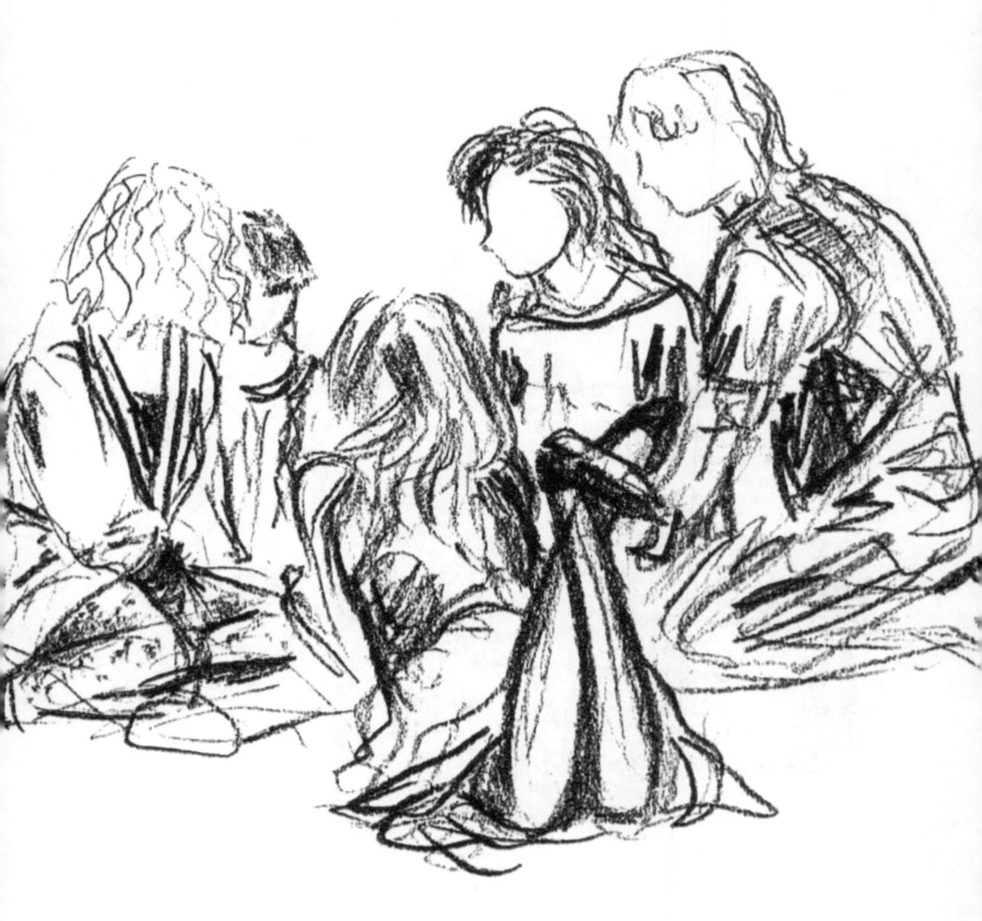

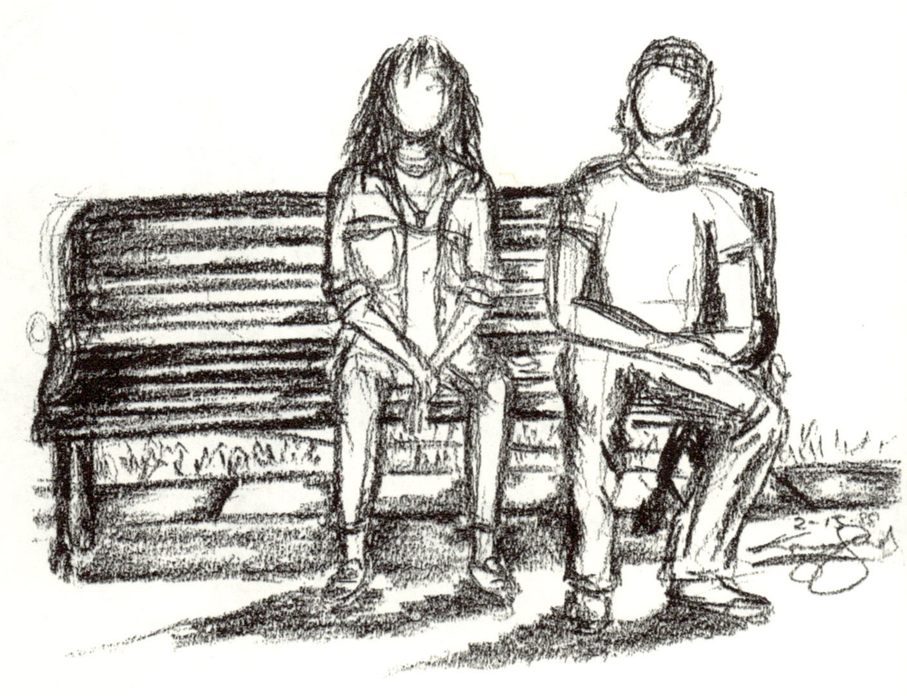

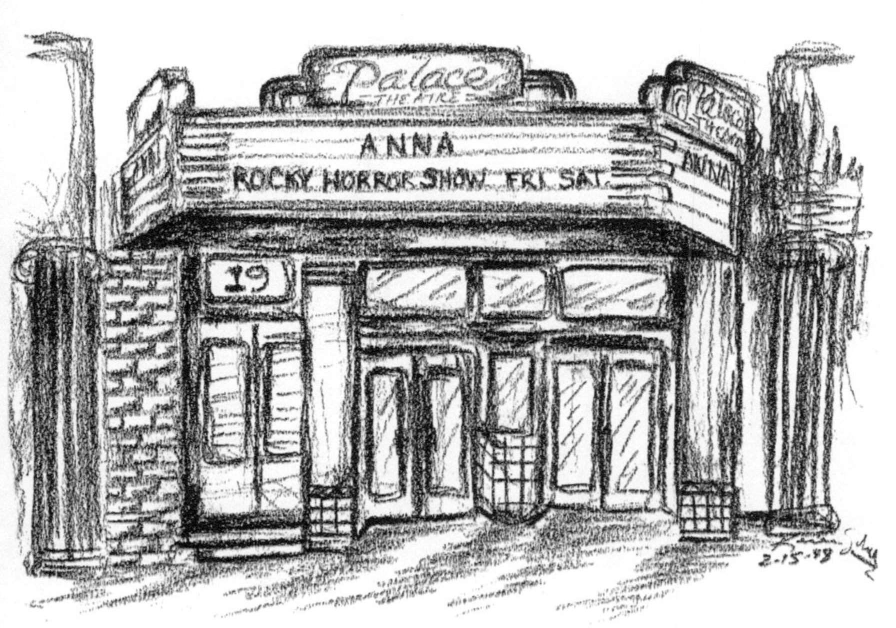
Palace
THEATRE
ANNA
ROCKY HORROR SHOW FRI SAT
19
Palace
THEATRE
ANNA
2-15-98

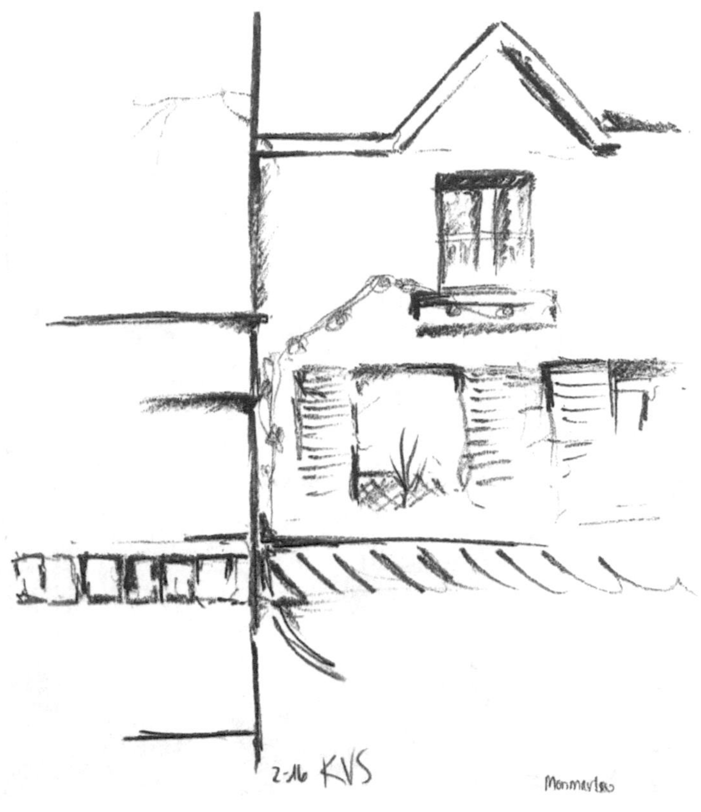

When I was eighteen, in 1989, I lived in Paris for four months. It was an influential place for me artistically and personally. It's peculiar how a place so different from where I grew up could resonate so deeply for me, but it did.

Paris

Paris Métro

A cantaloupe rolls across the subway floor
A tired man in a tattered coat picks it up,
walks across the moving car
and hands it back to the tired woman who lost it.
I sense a vulnerability in the man
something to do with his yellow teeth.

Another woman across the aisle with a backpack
and a small child looks at me
and I look back.
We look at each other
not with defensiveness, or camaraderie
just with our eyes.

My friend asks me something and
I turn to talk with her.
When I look back after a stop,
the woman and her child are gone.

I look out the window and see them on the platform.
We share a gaze as the train pulls out of the station.

The Restaurant

Five of us tumble into
the Greek restaurant
Quartier Latin
sparkling lights stone walls, wooden benches.

It's our first week here
and we really don't know French
or Greek
the menu indecipherable
to us.

We laugh at our predicament
and order random things
without knowing
what they are.

Imagine my surprise when the waiter brings me
a bowl of white sauce.
Then my friend receives a plate of pita
so we share.

Neils at Sacré Coeur

I was drawing Sacré Coeur
when I saw him, hair in his eyes, full lips.
He was putting makeup on
a beautiful woman's face.

I drew him I drew her
I drew the rest of their crew.
And then I went back to drawing
the street and the
towering white church
where I had just spent
most of Pâques
the previous Sunday
worshiping.

Then I heard him next to me
"Artiste?"
I looked up, smiled, and shrugged
"Peut être."

He spoke Dutch and English
not much French
and he took me with them
for the rest of the day.

Their photo shoot was over
the model went home.
It was him, the photographer
Ellie the wardrobe mistress
and me.

We wandered the streets,
napped in their hotel room and
went out to dinner
at a restaurant called 1912.

He took me home on the metro
late at night and kissed me
one more time
on the platform
before jumping on the last train.

I tried to go to 1912
again
a few weeks later.
But it wasn't there.

In France, Easter is called Pâques and is not only religious but a significant cultural holiday with a three-day weekend.

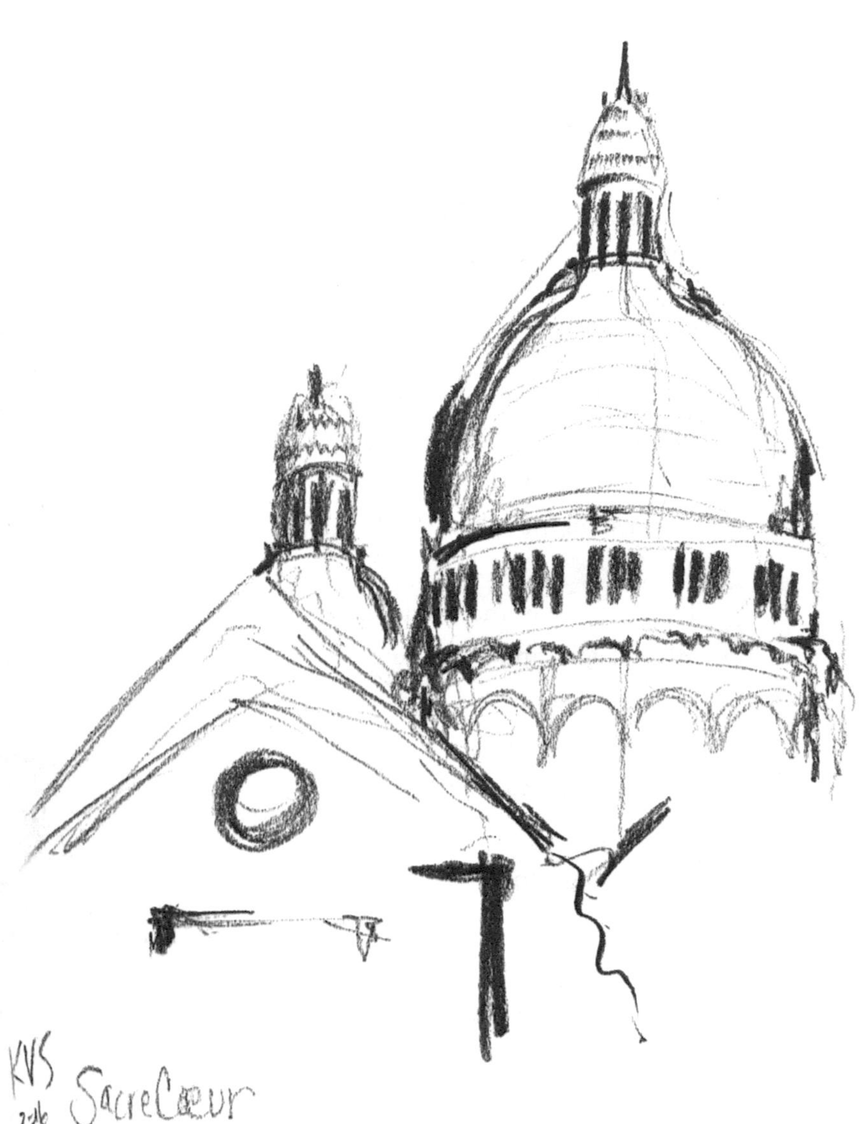

KVS
2016 SacreCœur

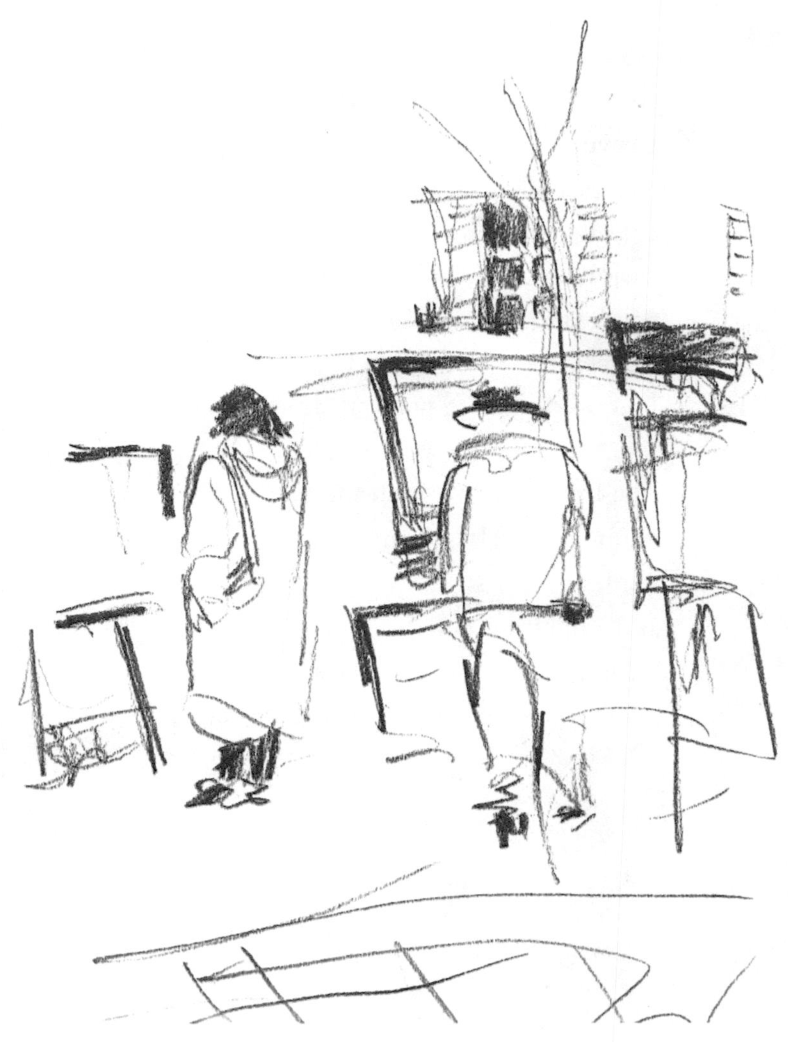

Shards

Glass blood
streaks across the floor of the bar.
I have holes in my stockings
and gashes in my feet
cut open silently
cleanly
painlessly.
I never knew
I enjoyed walking without shoes.

The broken bottle is cleaned up.
He pulls the glass from my feet
tenderly
and smiles.
"Comme ma souer," he says
pushing the hair from the side of my face.

Solitude

I went there at least a couple of times a week
feeling guilty that I should be seeing more of Paris
than just Beaubourg.
But I couldn't help it I loved
the strange architecture of the Centre Pompidou
the myriad performers on the huge cobbled plaza
with large steps
community space
music sunshine art lots of art
a Mattisse painting called Le Rêve
where I dreamed most days
inside and outside.
Library coffee and an art gallery
where I found the quietest artist I have ever met.
Van Hove — her paintings soft
like mornings in the country.
Quiet and I can't explain why I love her so much
or why she is inextricably tied to that place
a loud boisterous energy
where I could easily
drop into my solitude.

Le Rêve

Every week I visited
Le Rêve
I couldn't tell you why.

Something about her face
the strange green shadow on her arm
reflection from the artist's own blue quilt.

Maybe I just wanted
a reason to go into the
gallery.

I was in my own dream then
asleep but
sliding down a flattened plane.

Ugly shadows
a textured quilt background
claiming my right to see.

And the invisible images
behind eyelids
like fractals and infinite memories
multiplying.

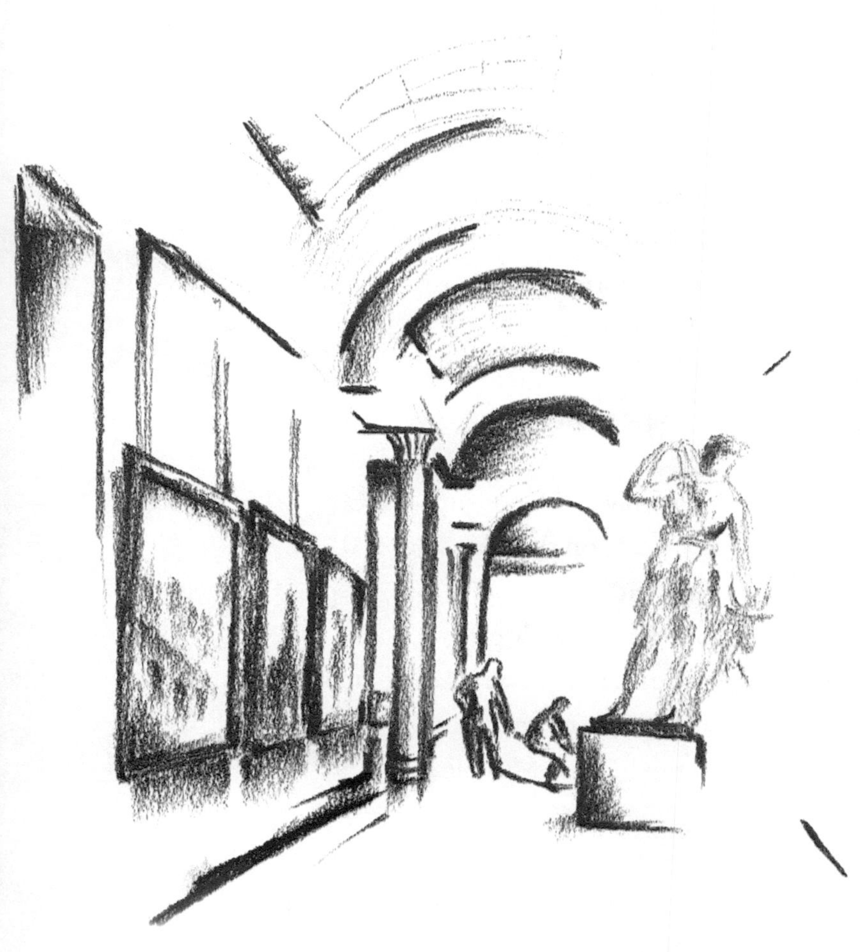
Louvre

The Pin

I.
In the Paris Métro stations
arts-and-crafts vendors
are everywhere.
Their cloth-covered tables
along the tunnel edges
offer up masterpieces
during rush hour.

It usually all blends into noise
my focus on the train ahead.
But that Tuesday
in the Chatelet Métro
one piece of jewelry catches my eye
on my way to board a train
to the Picasso Museum.

It's a pin made of flat clay pieces.
A woman in five simple colorful shapes
glued together.
Like a Picasso
two black circles for her breasts.
I don't even stop
but I see it and
I remember it.

II.
Three weeks later in the métro again
running for a train
a woman passes me going the other way.
She is wearing the pin.

I smile at the thought of her
stopping at the artist's table
buying that pin
and deciding to wear it that day
of all days
when I would walk past her
then and there.

III.
Two years later Kristine and I
are eating dinner at
Max's Diner in San Francisco.
Our waitress comes to take our order.
She is wearing the pin.
"Were you in Paris in 1989?" I ask.
Baffled, she says "Yes."

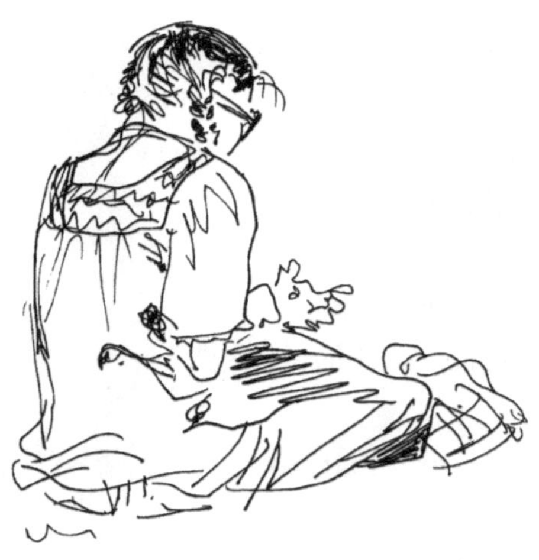

before a word forms

I lived in Utah in the early 1990s. It was where and when I became an adult. The dry mountainous landscape was very different from what I was used to in the coastal San Francisco Bay Area. My friends and I diligently went to our college classes, and also danced and drank in gay bars, lounged in Salt Lake City cafés, took road trips to New Mexico, made art, wrote, and some of us even eventually graduated.

Utah

Zion

Sean, Sue and I leave Provo
at 100 miles an hour
a radar detector on the dash
and arrive in Zion at night.

We unroll our beds then
roast tofu hot dogs
because Sue is vegan and
we are camping under infinite stars.

In the morning
I wake up shocked
by a Martian landscape.
I'm an alien under hot fiery cliffs
slicing a burning blue sky
I could never have imagined
a place like this.

Sue walks through the scarlet land
in ripped jeans
her head shaved and a ring
of tiny flowers
encircling a finger.
Sean follows

on the rusty path behind us
as we wander infinite crimson canyons.

We explore all morning
in reverance
then stop to cut a cantaloupe
on Sue's turtleneck
that she took off an hour ago
in the heat.

We eat the juicy melon and
toss the rinds
under the brush.

My hands and feet are red
I am part of this place now.

Melted on hot rocks
a red ant
crawls past my eye
then some kind of lizard
darts past my knee.
With all my effort
I lift myself off that rock.

We carve our way to the Virgin River
and Sue and I dip into it
so we can be virgins.

On the walk back
we sing until our breath
can only
be used to breathe.
That night Sean gets
sprayed by a skunk.

Silence sky sun
redrock sagebrush song
river ant lizard skunk
even us.

It could all be gone tomorrow.
But I keep forgetting.

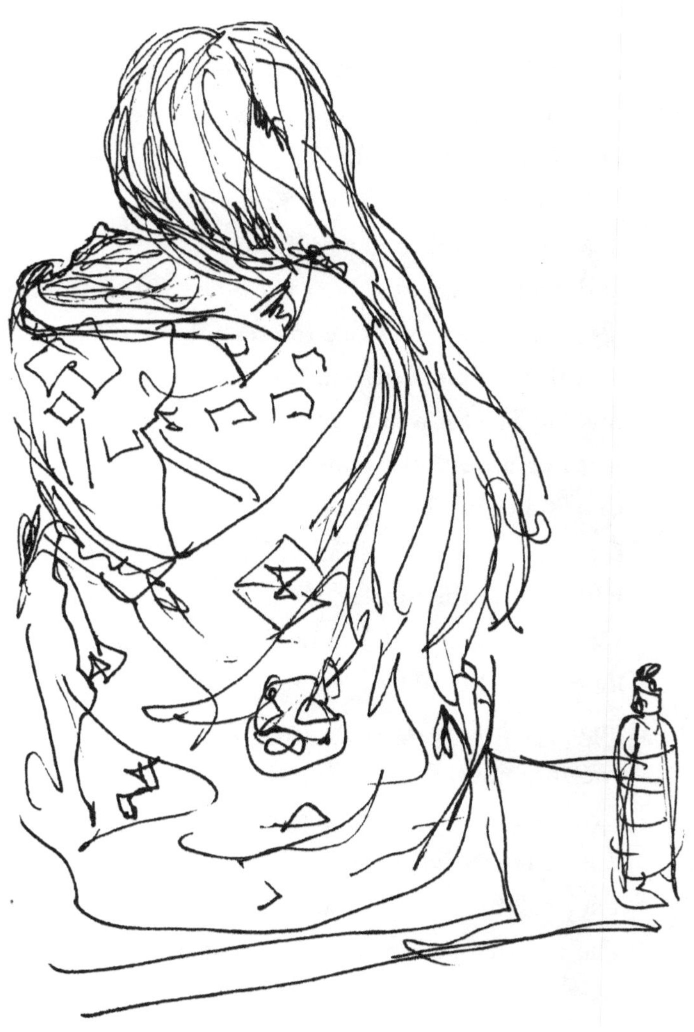

The Warlock

At the restaurant where I work in Provo,
the cook is an ex-con and smokes at the stove.
He offers me pot daily.
My coworkers and I make $2 per hour.
The place is attached to a motel
and while it serves a diner breakfast in the morning
it's a Chinese-food place the rest of the day.
I work the first shift, 6am to 11am,
making $10 for a morning of breakfast slinging and
working around the consistent stream
of roaches in the kitchen.
One of our regulars is an old guy
who lives at the motel.
He looks about sixty-five but is probably younger
long white blond hair, craggy face
huge gold hoop earrings and
two-inch-long fingernails.
He says he works construction on the railroad.
But I can't imagine it with those nails.
They call him the Warlock.
The rest of our customers are just passing through
just trying to get some breakfast before heading out.
They'll never be back, so why tip, most of them think.
But even though he is obviously broke
the Warlock always tips us well.

Heidie

We smoked a lot of pot at Heidie's.
We smoked cigarettes on the balcony.
We'd lean over the balcony
talking and would flick ashes absently and
the porch light of her apartment would buzz
on and off.

A small TV inside on the floor played videos
or something
and there was never any food
except maybe chips.

There were pills, pills of every color
in baggies stashed mostly in Vincent's room
I spent the night with him once and
we slept together on the living room floor.
But he wouldn't kiss me
because he was sick.

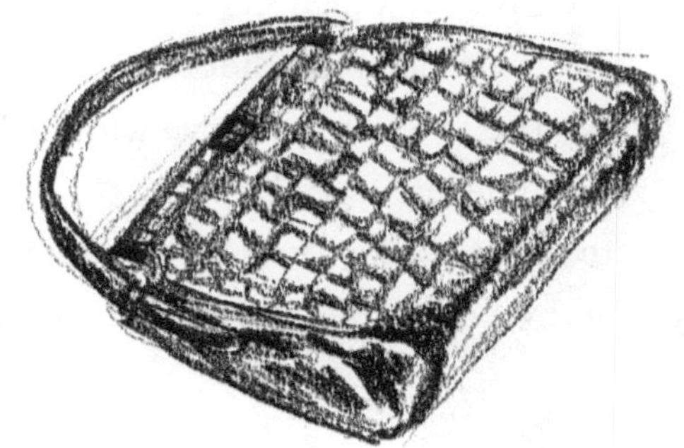

Winter in Utah

I lived mostly at night
on the streets and in dingy
apartments decorated with paintings and poems.
I remember a lot of light reflecting off the streets
light reflecting off rain and snow
clean cold presence very lonely.

I remember Jesse
thin and gray sunken cheeks,
sparse hair brushed upwards.
He dressed in long black pants and
long-sleeved black shirts
buttoned all the way up even in summer.
He was nineteen and anorexic
and we didn't do anything to help him.

The only thing he ate
was baby rice cereal
a few times a week.
He gave me a painting and a print that he made
and we walked to school together.
My friend Sue was in love with him.
Then he left school
to play the accordion he said
and we never heard from him again.

I might run into him in Germany
and we'll walk for hours
down stone streets in the rain
and we'll laugh and smile and think
how funny that we met here
after all these years.

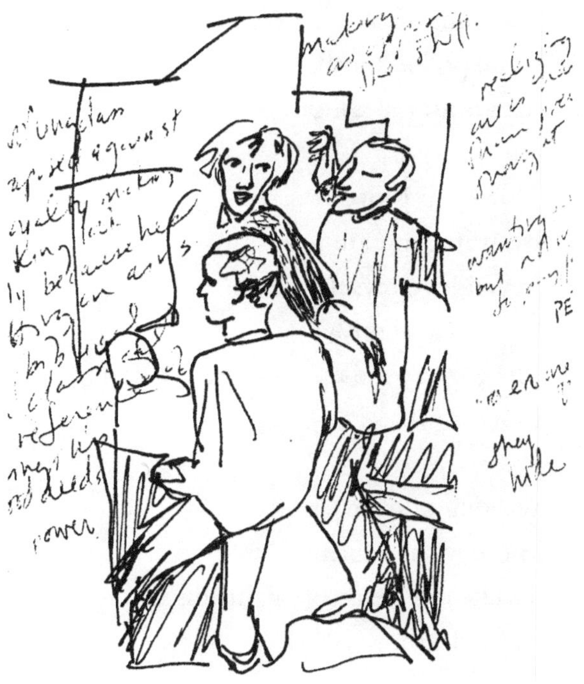

White Death

He came to see me but
was afraid to come into my house.
I went with him
and his friend.

Hair long black hair
everywhere
suffocating me.
Clothes scattered across a chaste floor
the scent of cloves floats in the air
while police spotlights
turn onto the window.

I love you I love you
Beautiful you are beautiful
I even love myself a little
he adds absently.
I love everyone do you love me
I love you.

Walking outside
in the white morning air,
it's like the death of night this is
white death.

You are beautiful in white death he says.

He gives me his hand and
white death takes us as
we walk down the pavement
wet from rain.

Come down here he says and
he leads me down a muddy path
under the street
where a violent river
is gushing past.
Look! he says and we look.
Life — rushing past us
is life.

Back up to the street to
try to ascend from this
underworld.
When we get to the street
he backs off
afraid.
The road and buildings contrast harshly
with the life of the river.

It's just cold dead edifice
and we are part of nature.
I'm scared (of civilization).

Now we are in the Denny's.
You look like you need coffee.
You are beautiful you are beautiful in white death.
We can make love just by looking at each other
he says in the middle of the Denny's.

I love everybody I'm so tired.
We go home we sleep.
I love you.
I love everyone.

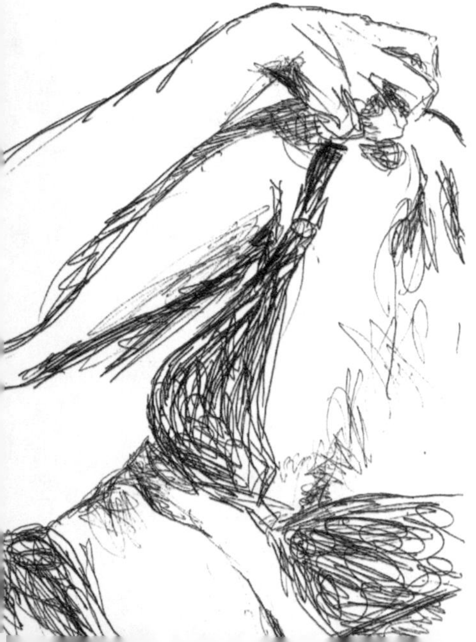

The Window

I remember walking
out a window
onto the roof at a party once.
I'm having a cigarette out there with Tamara
and some other people.
And then Tamara and I duck
through the window into the house again.

As I come through the window
I look up
and see a guy with long wavy golden hair.
He helps me into the house
and I kiss him because I realize
I love him.

I love him for a minute or two and
when I open my eyes Tamara is standing there
laughing and laughing.
I smile at the guy and he smiles back and
Tamara and I walk out
of the room
together.

Red Roads

I.
A gust of wind pushes us to Madrid.
Red roads
powdered chocolate donuts
chewing in our mouths.

An adobe church
carved clay saint in its tower
stands against a turquoise sky.
We stop, get out.
Graves lie
in front of the church.
They are covered in flowers and
surrounded by fences.
A little satin moon hangs
from one cross —
she died fifty years ago.

A dried chipmunk sprawls
in front of the chapel door
in dead weeds.
Friends hop cyclone fences to snap photos
in spite of warning signs that say
no trespassing, no photos.

II.
Driving down the red road I read a map.
We get to Madrid an old coal-mining town.
Inside a silver shop is a silversmith.
Weird jewelry, weird teeth and
he made the display cases
this one's from an old windshield.
Then an art gallery with hideous pillow sculptures
but he's doing exactly what he likes.

Outside on the muddy street
wind blows our hair into our teeth.
We find a bar to duck into.
"I Brake For Beer"
says a bumper sticker on a car outside.
Apparently.

III.
The four of us file in and sit down and order
beer and fries.
There's a guitarist playing songs from my dad's truck.
I look around the old saloon
horns decorate the place and money
tons of money hangs on the walls

and all the people
look like they're from a coal-mining town.

I go into the bathroom and a girl follows me in.
"You know when you walked in..." she starts
"What?" I say.
"It was beauty after beauty after beauty!" she laughs.
I go back to the table, tell Tamara and eat fries
sing along to the music and smoke.

Tamara goes up to the bar
where the girl from the bathroom is leaning.
"Did your friend tell you what I said?" she asks.
"Yeah, she did," says Tamara
and the girl laughs again.
"When you all walked in and around the table
I was like whoa!" she slaps her knee and laughs
again and her friends laugh with her.

When we go back to the car it's raining and there is mud
and we are singing country western and folk songs
through the sound of the wind.
We drive past a storm, a purple house and another
dog to Santa Fe.

Camille

I would walk every night
always alone
then I'd come home
to a red carpet and a bowl of bean soup that
Camille made the afternoon before
then we would talk and talk
about what I don't remember.

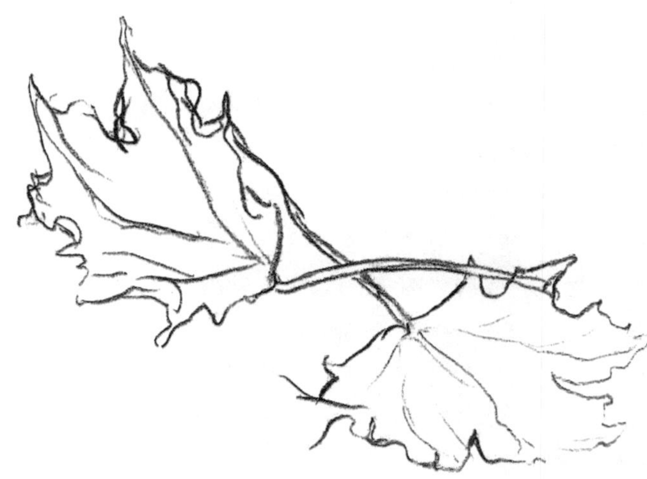

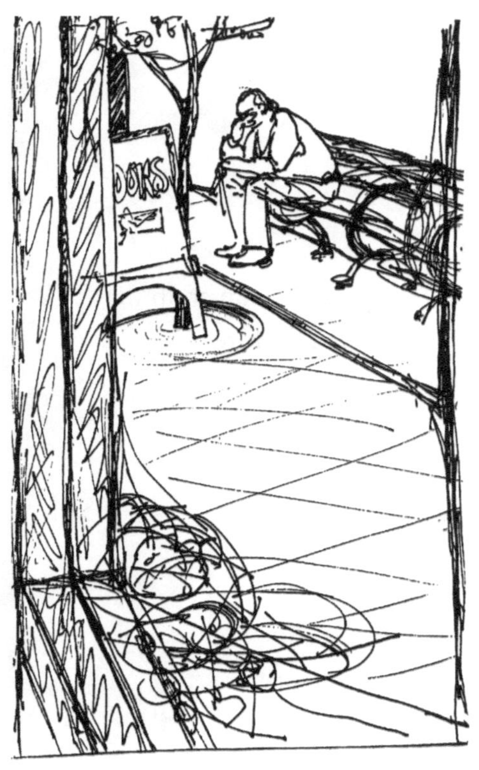

These poems were written about downtown
Petaluma and the nearby small town of Cotati,
where I worked in a clothing store in the early
1990s. Petaluma was full of cafés and places to
hang out, including Aram's Café and the Apple
Box. Some of these poems even began as ideas
there, where our generation lounged and met each
other daily. We wrote, drank copious amounts
of pourover coffee, espresso, and wine, and ate
Mediterraenean food alongside — and sometimes
with — older generations of artists, poets, and
random townies.

Downtown Petaluma

The Apple Box Café

We carry our coffee outside
to sit at a table, speaking French
when a train goes by.

The sound drowns out our speech for a minute
as the grinding metal cars glide over the trestle
built along the waterfront in 1922.

It used to be grain
and eggs here
transported out of town
to San Francisco
before the Golden Gate.

Now this trestle hosts cups of pourover coffee
(before anyone did pourover coffee).

I am always shocked that I can sit
inches away from an active train
and drink a latte.

But it's the 1990s
and we are all in in our twenties
and we don't even realize how happy we are.

The Women

At the café exit
suburban women push
purposefully
out the door
then walk all over town
in their husbands' shirts
carrying babies like
cumbersome handbags.

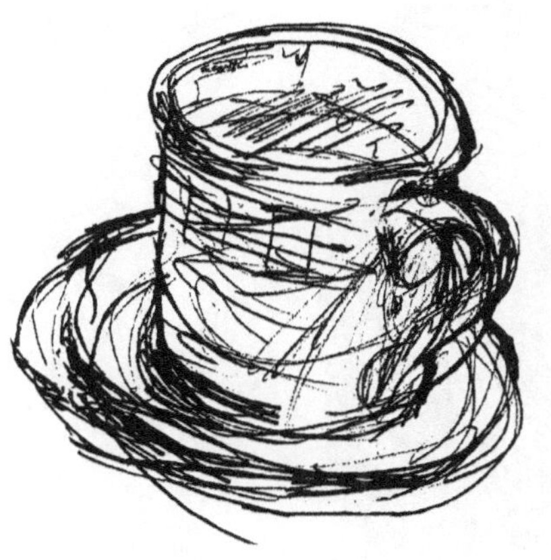

Waitress

Sometimes
it is necessary
to drink to excess
like a periodic release
from silent hysteria.

Smiling girl walks by
and the seven-year waitress
leans over the table
short skirt and apron
compromising her
authority.

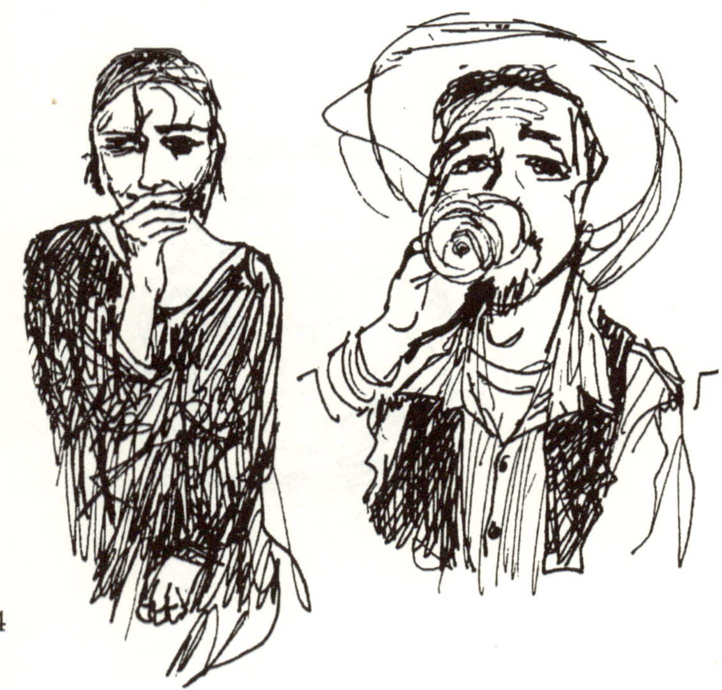

The Butterflies

Two girls walk past the window.
They look beaten down.
They look triumphant.

One wears striped stockings and
a flowered dress.
The back of the dress is
completely hiked up
under her backpack.
Oblivious
she walks up the stairs with her friend
and disappears into the parking garage.

Then come the butterflies.
They fly in and out of the dark café
and no one notices them but me.

Was I the only one
who noticed the girl's skirt?
Would she ever even know?
Would she walk along until
she sat down somewhere
took off her backpack, lit a cigarette
then got up and went on her way
dress in its proper place?

Couple

Outside the café
the sidewalk falls inward
broken yet
they sit there anyway
at the small table and chairs
teetering on the cement edge.
She leans forward to give
her order
and he
looks up at her
every movement.

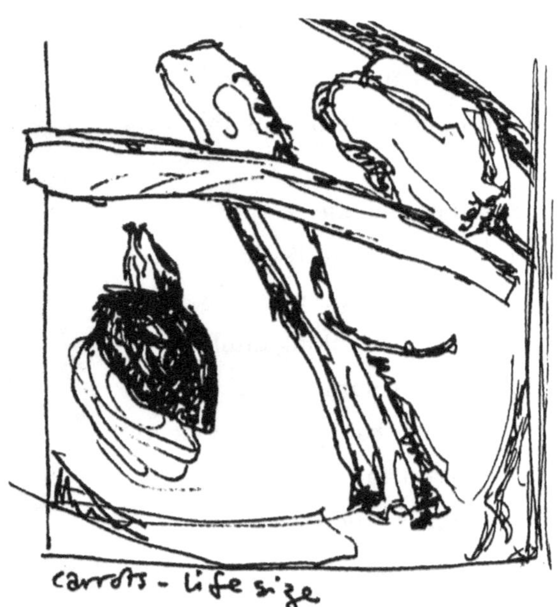

The Bookstore

It's seven-thirty
and I walk to Arams Café
to drink coffee and write and read books
for an hour and a half.

I'm waiting for my husband
to close the used bookstore
across the street at nine
so we can walk home together.

But really
I love having this alone time.

Sometimes
I go into the bookstore early
and quietly peruse the books
on homesteading
and self-sufficiency
and gardening
as if I don't live in
an apartment
on Petaluma Boulevard.

The Clothing Store

The scent of garbage belts across
the clothing store
where I work in Cotati.
The mail truck rolls by
outside display windows
where clothes hang with their dead beauty
waiting to be animated.

This morning my eyes are heavy red
and the man who walks
shoots-up into his hand
behind the building
and later punches someone in the face.

The homeless man on the corner
comes in to use the mirror.
He tells me he is going to Hawaii.

That afternoon I see him playing the piano at
the Inn of the Beginning across the street.
A gust of wind comes in
and blows his sheet music
across the room.
He keeps playing.

The street rises up to
make a wall and we crash into it
amidst leaning trees
at sixty miles an hour.

Low music throbs through the building walls
sending secret messages
and two weeks later
I receive a postcard at the store
from Hawaii.

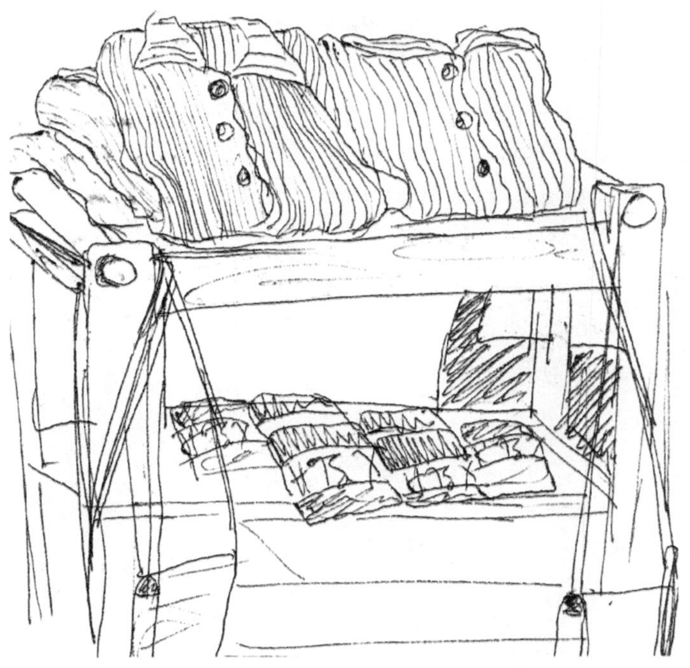

Ladies

There they are again
those two old ladies
black jackets silk scarves
around their hair
clasping arms
in the cold biting air of late winter
as they descend the curb together.

A large tear rolls down
one woman's face and
smiling at each other
their black pumps step deliberately down.

They are of the Old World when
people clasped arms and
wore silk scarves around their hair.

I pass them and
step up
onto the broken curb.

Her Cake

Outside the café
the birds
nibbled on her cake
and she didn't notice.

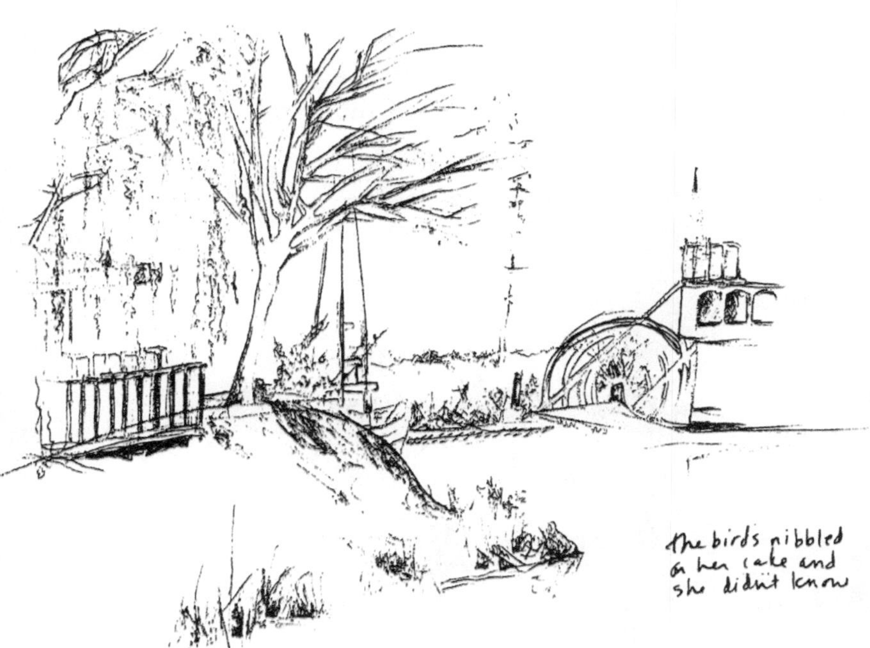

Sugar

The individual packet of sugar
is wasteful.
They exist because
everyone wants their own.
No communal sugar bowl for us.
The people who use sugar
always seem to need
four or five packages of the stuff
leaving the empty papers
scattered on café tables
like urban leaves.

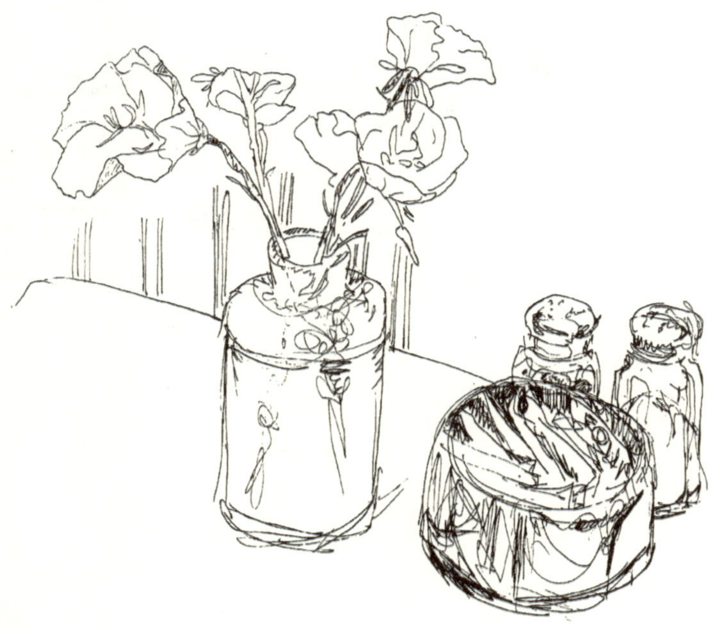

Alienation

I.
He went down into the alley
and they didn't talk
and then he went back upstairs.
Alone.

II.
I could stay here all night drinking
in the darkness of a small but familiar city.
I down the last of the wine and grit my teeth.
Aram's wine is teeth-gritting.

III.
Do I still need to write about
alienation
or am I finally at home?

Paper Napkin

It falls down
over and under
glides towards the floor
at knee height
towards her tall friend
who tentatively gives haircuts
to random friends and
acquaintances
in front of the café.

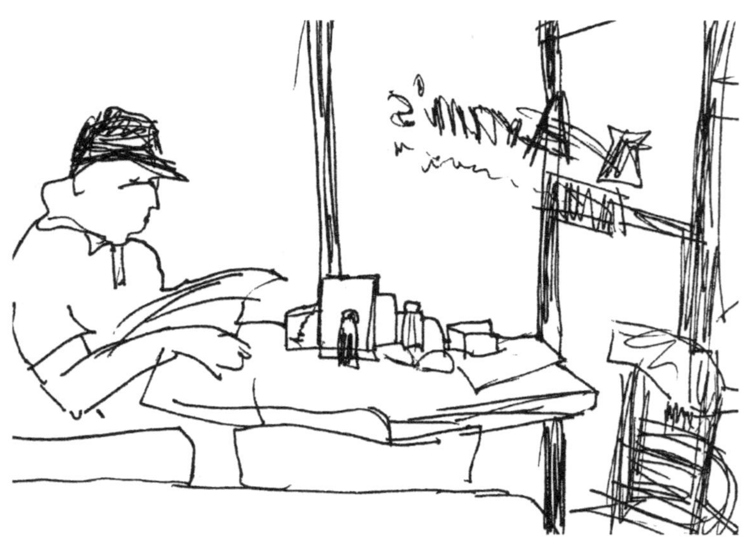

Daisy

I would write but
there's nothing much going on.
It's that time, almost six
when everyone is barely home
from work and they aren't going out yet.
I sit at a table outside.
Across the street the Hideaway
is slowly sparking to life and
I order drinks for Kelly and me.
She is coming here tonight
to pick up her dog.
When she moved this week
the dog disappeared
like they sometimes do
after a move.
But instead of returning to the old house
the dog came here
to the café.
Walking three and a half miles
and crossing a freeway
and the river.
"Oh Daisy," Kelly says when she arrives
and Bruce leads the dog still wet
to our table.
"What are we going to do with you?"

An Historical Context

In the nineties
when the art professor asked me
How do you describe your work
in an historical context?
I thought
What historical context? and
What work?

I watched
drew
painted
wrote.
There was no context
no body of work.
Just endless musings and sketches
of what I saw.

Outside the café
an old man helped his wife
who had one leg
into the car.

He seemed to love her and
didn't even look at

the young woman
across the street
buying frozen yogurt.
Time and circumstance had
changed his priorities.

Would we continue to sit at Aram's?
Year in and year out?
I watched the weather moving outside
and tried to think about my work
in an historical context.

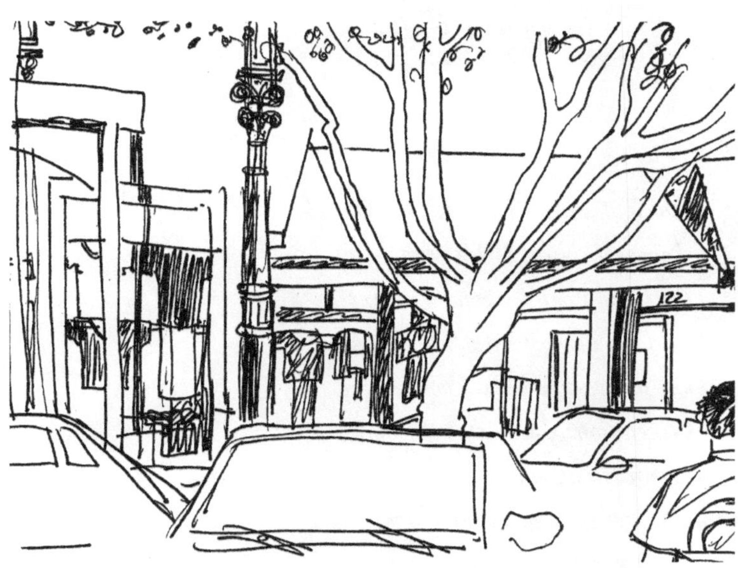

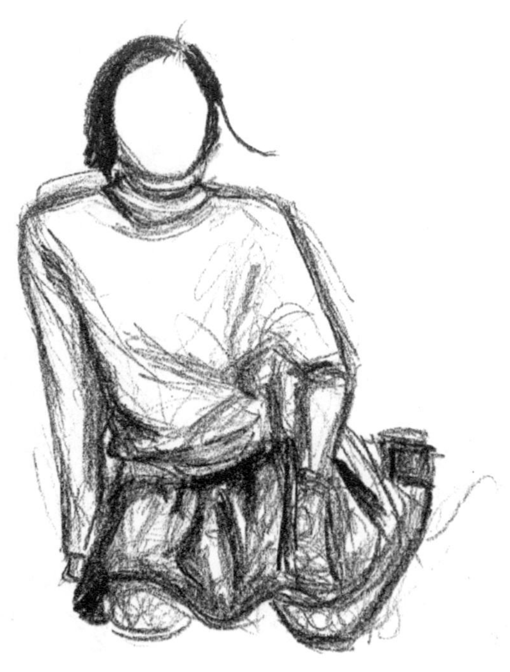

On September 11, 2001, the tone of the world changed. We were about thirty, and besides living in a new world, a new generation had arrived, one to rival the baby boom in size. Generation X was now the smallest generation on earth, even more X than before, sandwiched between two massive markets of consumers.

The Turn of a Century

The Day After

In 1999 my generation
partied like Prince suggested.
It was the Turn of the Century
a once-in-a-lifetime experience and Y2K
was about to go very wrong
the powers-that-be warned us
due to a tiny-but-significant computer glitch.
So what, we thought.
We've heard it before.

Born from the American Dream
but just after its passing
Generation X had always been told
"You'll see wonders in your lifetime
picturephones, jetpacks, maybe even time travel."
But on the other hand they said
"The entire world will probably end
in a nuclear explosion."

In 1983 we got extra credit in school
to watch a movie on TV
about how nuclear holocaust was going to go.

The day after in class
Chris F asked the teacher

"OK, so what do we do?"
and the teacher looked at him and said
"There's nothing you can do."

We lived our lives knowing this.
And here we were still around
the Turn of the Century imminent
a story we had heard somewhere and now
it was coming to us.

The last century had brought
cars, airplanes, computers, at least two world wars
and a flu pandemic.

We wondered if we would finally see wonders.
But we knew from the movies that utopian thinking
had already given way
to dystopia.

The morning of January 1, 2000
was strangely quiet
and everything seemed fine.
My husband went outside for a cigarette,
looked around and asked
"Where's the robots?"

Storm

Rain rain rain I crash through
water on my way home
flash floods words blinding
rain covers eyes.

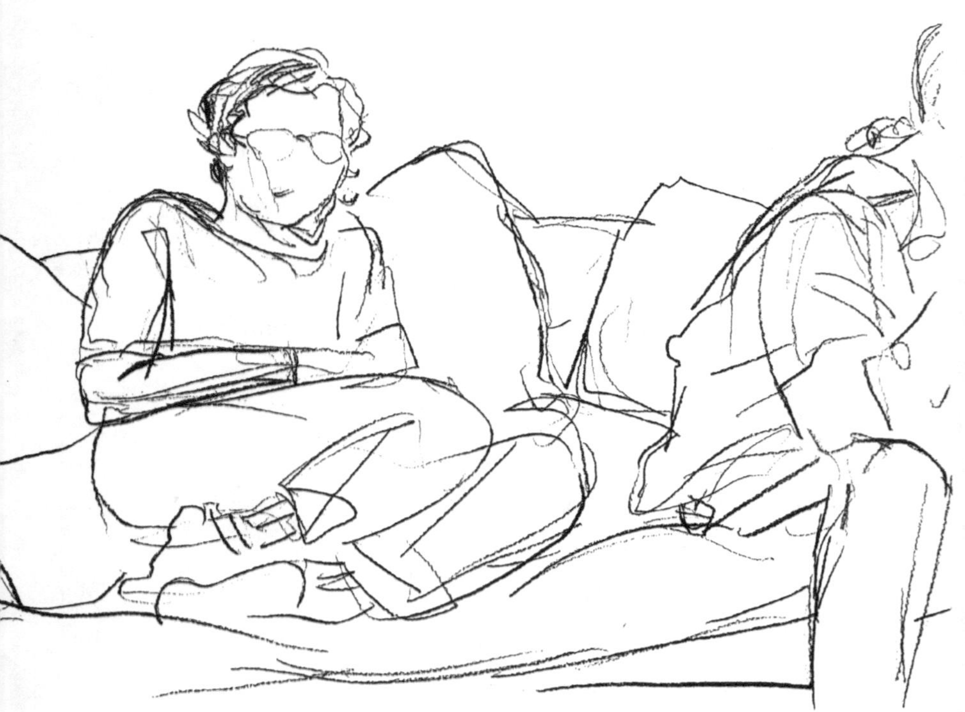

Youth

A brigade of clean, long-haired
youth
wearing ripped jeans
goes by the café window.
They play at being homeless.
Being moderately fucked-up
is not in fashion.
You must be
very fucked-up
or else
completely satisfied.

Wine Country

I wake up
gray weather
ants in the sink
of my Boulevard apartment.
I turn on all the lights
trying to make it seem
like day.

When I arrive at work
on the other side of the freeway
where we print wine labels
for the vast grape empires
in California and Oregon
the presses aren't running.

And instead of setting up art for
syrah, chardonnay and zinfandels
we go to a meeting where we are told
there will now be a time clock because
Darren has been coming in ten minutes late.

How did we end up here?
I whisper to Brenda during the meeting.
She pauses before answering
"It was a fluke."

But I wonder.

Chemicals and ammonia
choke the press room where we are meeting
but no one seems to notice.

"What is that smell?"
I ask JoAnn the manager.
She looks puzzled and says
"I don't smell anything."
And then I watch her walk away.

I walk away too.

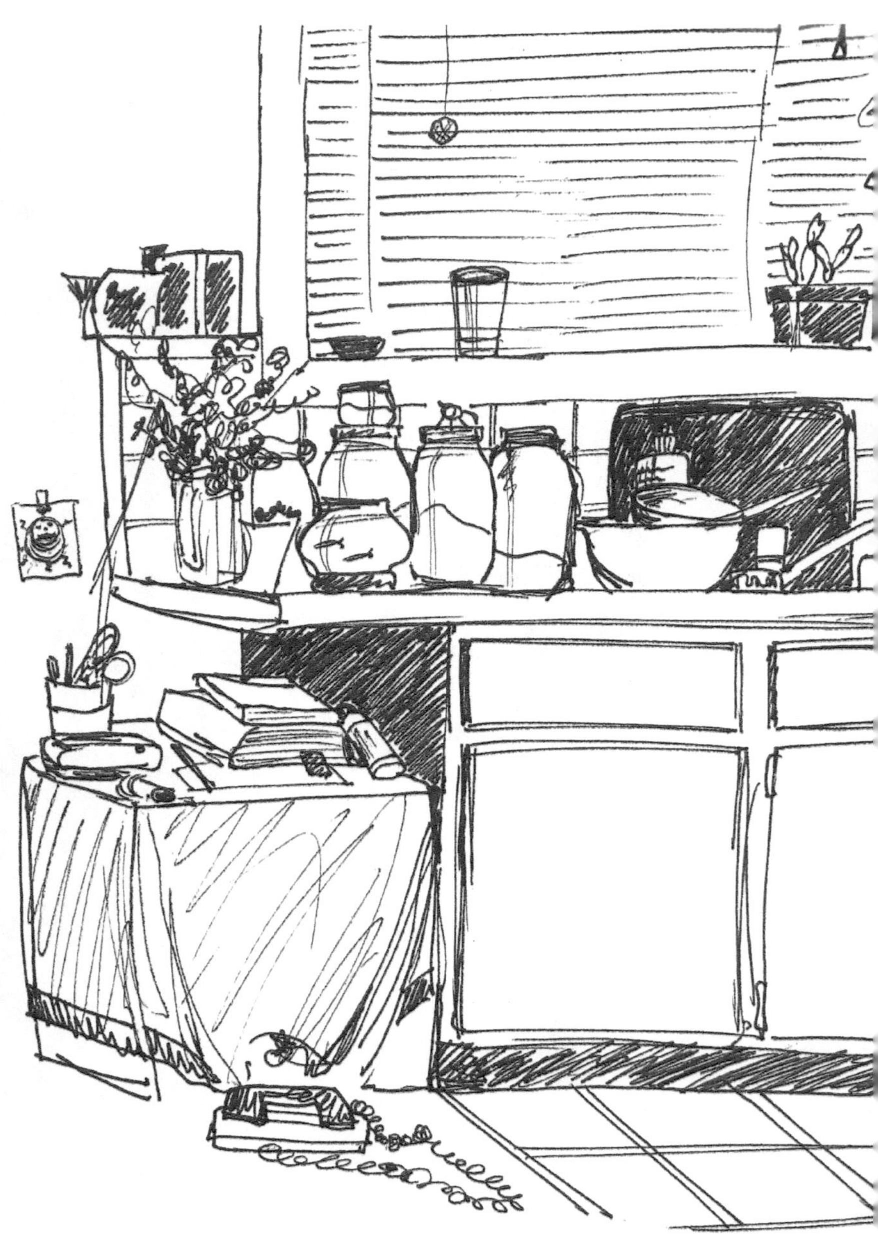

Things That Cover the Table

Wrappers from different kinds of chocolate bars.
Bookmarks or things
that could end up as bookmarks.
Mugs with a little bit of coffee at the bottom.
Piles of crystals and stones.
Papers that I need to get to.
Scraps of paper with notes scrawled on them
that I don't recall writing
that make me remember a dream.
Burnt matches.

Smoke

Partial darkness obscures her face
Light fades towards black and she
becomes more and more shadowy
approaching me with
desert sagebrush smouldering
in an abalone shell.

Sweet smoke fans through the air
towards me
over me
around me
and all the others in this darkening room
sealing and protecting us
with the feathers of a bird.

Thoughts and actions originate and end
implicated
in certain sections of our brains
but science can't say where
the thought process itself takes place.

Where does that energy go
after a thought begins
and before it ends?

Could it be carried by smoke?

The haze is thick now
and I glow in the luminescence of
near night in fall
cleansed healed lighter
in seconds.

I hadn't realized how heavy I had felt
these past few days
when all that we saw
over and over
were towers of endless smoke
the clouds bigger
than the buildings.

The night before
I dreamt of skyscraping edifices
destroyed by flooding
an ocean crashing through
knocking out walls and arches behind me
barely escaping again and again
while I run
through a billion tears.

And when I wake up and
turn on the kitchen radio
my dream is real

and I wonder
if the anticipatory thoughts of those men
wandered around
flooding our dreams that night
with metaphors
of water and weeping.

Cedar White Sage Desert Sagebrush
Tobacco Kopal Frankincense
and more much more.

Perfume
para fume
with smoke.
We rarely see
one thing
transmute into another.

But with smoke
simple matter shifts

into transparent veils of white blue pink
an acting messenger
intermediary between us
and them.

"Smoke," she says, holding the abalone shell.
"It's not quite stuff, and it's not quite nothing."

It's a transformative moment
a sacrificial offering.

*This poem was inspired by a lecture on Sacred Smoke by
ethnobotanist Kat Harrison in Sebastopol, California. The
lecture happened to have been scheduled two days after the
events of September 11, 2001, which transmuted our reality
in seconds.*

Epilogue

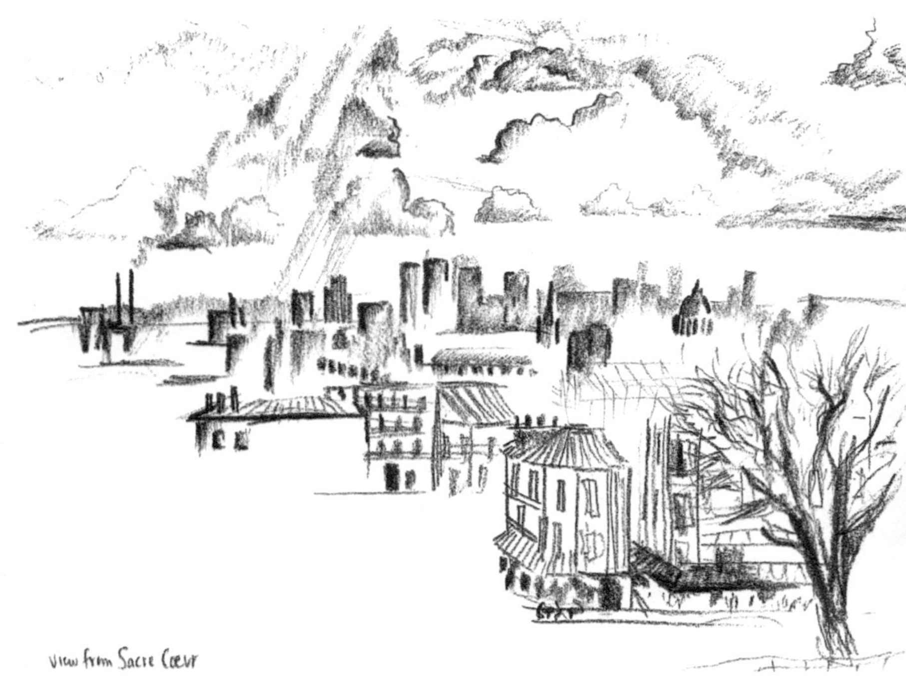

view from Sacre Coeur

How I Remember

These memories are like dreams
already almost gone
in the morning of age.
When I try to remember a face
it shifts
and I discover
that it doesn't matter how I remember
or if I remember
what happened
as long as the feeling I had then
is still there.

About the Author

Kary Hess is an artist and author. She has a BA in Art from Brigham Young University and is currently pursuing an MFA in Interdisciplinary Arts at California Institute of Integral Studies. She is the creator and author of the SparkTarot® deck and guidebook, is a graphic designer and painter and writes for San Francisco Bay Area alternative newsweeklies and magazines. She lives with her family in Petaluma, California.